'13

W9-CYT-726

WITHDRAWN

# INTERNSHIP & VOLUNTEER OPPORTUNITIES

## for TV and Movie Buffs

Adam Furgang

ROSEN
PUBLISHING®

New York

Published in 2013 by The Rosen Publishing Group, Inc.
29 East 21st Street, New York, NY 10010

Copyright © 2013 by The Rosen Publishing Group, Inc.

First Edition

**Library of Congress Cataloging-in-Publication Data**

Furgang, Adam.
Internship & volunteer opportunities for TV and movie buffs/Adam Furgang. — 1st ed.
      p. cm. — (A foot in the door)
Includes bibliographical references and index.
ISBN 978-1-4488-8295-3 (library binding)
1. Motion pictures—Vocational guidance. 2. Television—Vocational guidance. 3. Volunteer workers in the arts. 4. Internship programs. I. Title.
PN1995.9.P75F87 2013
791.4302'93—dc22

2012014792

*Manufactured in the United States of America*

CPSIA Compliance Information: Batch #W13YA: For further information, contact Rosen Publishing, New York, New York, at 1-800-237-9932.

# Contents

CASTING →

If you are interested in television and film, take any opportunity you can to learn about the business. Acting is a fun way to learn about how productions are made.

# Introduction

Some people seem to love TV and movies more than others. They might quote their favorite movies all the time, or they might know the behind-the-scenes details of their favorite shows. Movie and TV buffs come in all varieties. Some hope to become actors, writers, cinematographers, or directors, while others dream of working anywhere in the industry just to be around something they love. For those who want to become involved in the industry, there are plenty of opportunities.

Careers can take a lifetime to build, but there are many things that young people can do to explore the entertainment, media, and communications industry. Internship and volunteer opportunities can help teens learn what it is like to work in film or television so they can decide if they want to pursue it as a career.

An internship is an experience in which a student or other kind of trainee works at a company or organization to learn about the field. Internships are often unpaid work experiences; some offer academic credits in high school or college. Many companies have organized internship programs that are designed to help interns learn different parts of the business while they provide help to the regular staff.

A volunteer opportunity is one that is offered without pay, and it may be less organized or structured than an internship. Either way, a person taking part in an internship or volunteer opportunity in the TV or film industry stands to gain valuable experience and learn a lot about the field, as well as make helpful contacts. People who take part in these opportunities often have an advantage when searching for employment when they are ready to start their careers.

There are many areas of the communications field that are worthwhile for a TV or film buff to explore. In the field of television, there are great opportunities available at local news stations, in public television, and in cable television. In the world of movies, there are production companies, documentary film companies, and special effects postproduction companies that may offer opportunities to young people.

There are also many opportunities in the field that do not involve working on film or TV shows directly. Jobs outside production include working at movie studios that are open to the public or working with talent agencies and casting companies. In addition, there are many industry magazines, film institutes, museums, and advertising firms that young people can explore to get a flavor of the film and TV industry before jumping headfirst into a career.

So take the time to explore what kinds of opportunities might be available based on your geographic location, your school schedule, and your interests. As an intern or volunteer, you may find that you are getting a great head start on an interesting and rewarding career. Or you may discover early that the field is not for you. Either way, you will be sure to learn something important through the many internship or volunteer opportunities for TV and movie buffs.

# Chapter One

# WHY INTERN OR VOLUNTEER?

The first thing that a teenager should know about starting a volunteer or internship program is that you will likely be given simple, low-level tasks to begin with. You can't expect to work at a movie studio and immediately chat with A-list stars or be included in important discussions about the special effects, the budget, or even the catering menu. You probably won't be involved in planning how to do Brad Pitt's hair. The work of an intern or volunteer is much more humbling. You might spend weeks cleaning up the catering table, getting coffee for people, or loading the special effects truck before going out to help the crew get that perfect shot of a sunset. You might be asked to answer phones or stuff envelopes that will be sent to people who auditioned for a television show.

The jobs of interns and volunteers are the lowest on the totem pole, and their names often fly by in the credits at the speed of light—if they are put in the credits at all. So why do people take these jobs? The answer is plain and simple: they

Television and film productions involve a lot of behind-the-scenes teamwork from camera and sound crews. You can observe some of this work as an intern or volunteer.

can be the ticket to your future. What you do and learn in internships or volunteer opportunities counts as pure experience. You're not subject to layoffs or budget cuts, and people in the field are getting to know you. That's great news if you want to continue to work in the field in the future. Here are some of the most convincing arguments for taking a job as an intern or volunteer in the film or television field.

## Get to Know the Field

Although as an intern or volunteer you will probably not be doing the work you want to do for life, the experience can be invaluable. Sure, you might be photocopying or running errands, but think of the setting you will be working in. The film and TV industries are among the most glamorous in the world. You could very well be on a set with famous people, and you will be learning about the world they work in. Just by being

Many film crews travel and work all around the world. This crew is working on location in the desert in California. The boom operator places the microphone.

present, you will learn about how people in the industry work, what kinds of jobs they do, and why these jobs are important in the field.

While working in the field, you may become fascinated with jobs that you didn't even know existed. You may be surprised to learn about the person who holds the microphone above the actors' heads, or the person who hooks up the microphone packs for actors to wear during filming. You may be shocked to learn how long actors must sit in the hair and makeup department before going in front of the camera and how this affects the entire production schedule. The more you learn, the more you understand the field, the productions, and what it takes to get the work done. Getting to know the field at a young age will help you make more informed career decisions and will likely make you a more valuable employee in the future.

Working in the field as an intern or volunteer will give you the opportunity to decide what part of the industry interests you the most. Interns and volunteers usually have less pressure, so they can think about and assess the field as a whole. For example, you may be able to speak with employees about their jobs and what they like about them. You may learn what makes a company's particular production similar to or different from others. As an intern or volunteer, you definitely have a job to do and to take seriously, but you also have the luxury of soaking in the knowledge that you gain as a temporary worker who is new to the scene. You can learn what you like and don't like about the field. You can use this knowledge when it is time to look for a college or your first paying job in the field.

## Change Your Mind If You Want

It may not seem like you have a luxurious job when you are in the middle of a hot movie set or giving a tour of an old movie lot, but you

# Show Initiative

Even though you may be the least experienced person in the room, show that you are a fast learner. Although you are not ready to start working in the field full-time yet, making good connections now can help you when you are looking for work or recommendations down the road. Take the work seriously and your boss or supervisor will take you seriously. Get to work on time, and dress appropriately. Ask good questions. If you don't have much to do, ask what else you can do to help. People who show initiative and maturity are far more valuable to an employer than someone who has to be reminded to do his or her job or to stop horsing around. Treat your internship as one of the most important things that you do.

actually have a lot of freedom. An intern or volunteer is not yet set on an official career path. You can change your mind if you decide that the experience is not for you. If the business you are interning or volunteering in is not what you thought it would be, you have the luxury of choosing another one and taking advantage of another internship or volunteer opportunity in an area you might enjoy more.

Film and TV interns work in offices as well as on production sets. Whatever you are asked to do, show a positive attitude and strive to exceed the employer's expectations.

You should definitely finish any internship or volunteer job you start: you are building a reputation no matter what job you are doing. But if you decide that you want to move from the television world to the film world, or even move from the film world to become a veterinarian, it's not a big deal. You will have learned something new about the world of work. You will have gained valuable "soft skills," including how to handle yourself in a professional setting. If you are unsure about your ideal career, identifying what you *don't* want to do can be a valuable step in learning what you *do* want to do.

## Learn About College or Training

Having an internship or volunteer opportunity before college is a unique situation for many students. As a high school student, you still have the chance to decide where you want to go to college or technical school and what you want to study. An internship or volunteer opportunity can help you learn what you want to focus on after high school. As a result, you can research the best colleges or technical programs for your interests.

As you intern or volunteer, talk with employees. Find out where they went to school and what they majored in. You may learn about some good programs in communications, film, or television production that you might want to research further. It helps to chat with any employees about their education, but asking the people closest to your age will yield the most recent information. You may even be able to take advantage of some of the same classes or teachers that those just out of college can recommend to you.

## Build a Great College Application

Completing an internship or volunteer job can help with the process of applying to and getting into the college of your choice. Real-world experience is valuable and looks great on a college application. College acceptance committees look for students who take initiative and make an effort to get involved and learn things on their own.

Colleges know that at this age, students who take internships and volunteer opportunities are driven and self-directed learners. This is always a plus on a college application. In addition, having real-world experience to write about in a college application essay or include in a portfolio is a real benefit to an applicant. An internship experience will make your college application stand out among the piles of applications that are being considered. This may very well expand your choices about where you go to college.

Remember that an internship is not a free ticket into college, however. You must also keep up your grades as you intern or volunteer. That will demonstrate that you can be a balanced and dedicated student who can handle the academic workload while also pursuing your future career.

# Chapter Two

# HOW TO LAND
# THE RIGHT GIG

I f you have decided that you'd like to try an internship or volunteer program in television or film, it's important to look in the right places for the right opportunities. While most of the high-profile work is done in Los Angeles and New York City, there are thousands of television stations and film houses across the country that can offer great opportunities for students willing to work hard and learn. In fact, local organizations may be more willing to give a high school intern a chance, since they are less likely to be deluged with inquiries from college students.

Since you will likely need permission from a parent or guardian to do the job, it makes sense to involve your parents in the process from the start. They can help you decide if you can get transportation to the job and if you can handle the workload along with your schoolwork. The financial aspect of the job is also something worth talking about with parents. Can your family afford to have you take a job with no pay or one that only offers academic credits? If you can work these things out with your family, you can begin your search for the opportunity that best fits your interests. Stay positive. You just might find what you are looking for.

## Keep an Eye Out

One of the best ways to find a volunteer position or internship is to identify companies that may be looking for help. Your school's guidance office may have a list of organizations that work with high school students through volunteer or internship programs. Look through

Internships and volunteer programs are great opportunities to meet people in the field and discover what they do. You may come away from the experience learning even more than you expected.

these files and talk to your guidance counselor about opportunities related to film and television. He or she may be familiar with media organizations that have worked with students in the past.

Even if you don't have a major movie set nearby, just about every city has a local news station or a newspaper with an entertainment section. These are places you can target for possible opportunities. Write a letter to these local media organizations, telling them that you are looking for volunteer or internship opportunities. With a little bit of research, you can uncover additional opportunities in your area. For example, your librarian may be able to help you develop a list of local film and video production companies. Look for organizations that interest you, and then write to them expressing your interest.

Be sure to let the organizations know that you are in high school. While many television stations and production companies offer internships to college students, they may not have the same programs for younger people. They may have to follow laws regarding the ages of people they hire to do certain jobs. Be sure to follow these rules and give the employer the chance to follow them as well.

Check the newspaper for publicized job opportunities. Companies sometimes advertise when a film crew is visiting town to do location shoots. It may be cheaper for the company to hire local help than to pay to bring people on location. Instead of paying for the food and lodging of their regular

Looking for advertised openings and calling companies is a good way to learn which organizations use interns and volunteers and what you can expect from the job.

studio workers, they may advertise for local help to get them through a scene.

Look for help needed at film festivals as well. Festivals as large as the Sundance Film Festival or as small as a high school event require help from interns and volunteers.

On the Web, you may find companies that specialize in finding work opportunities and internships for teens. Be careful to find out

# Interviewing: Preparation and Etiquette

As a high school student, the interview process for landing an internship or volunteer opportunity will probably not be as rigorous as it would be for someone seeking permanent employment. However, students should still be prepared to speak confidently with someone about the position. They should be able to communicate clearly why they want the position and what they think they can offer the company as an intern or volunteer. It's a good idea to write down your ideas beforehand. Then practice with a parent or teacher until your statements feel natural.

After someone gives you an interview, remember to thank that person, regardless of whether or not the interview results in a job. The person took time out of a busy schedule to talk with you, and you should recognize and appreciate that. A formal written letter that is sent through the mail is best, but an e-mail thank-you note can also be effective. In the thank-you note, you can repeat your interest in interning

ahead of time if these companies charge fees or if there are age restrictions involved.

## Go with Who You Know

There's a saying: "It's all in who you know." When it comes to contacting people at your top-choice companies, that can certainly be

at the organization. While it is certainly necessary to thank the person as the interview ends, taking the extra step of sending a note will help you make the right impression.

Interviews are a great chance to learn about a company. Even if you do not land a job or internship, you can ask questions about the industry and make a good impression.

the case. If you happen to know any people in the film or television industry, ask them if they know of any opportunities that young students can take advantage of. It may give you a great chance to get your foot in the door. People really do provide favors to friends or family, or even the friends of friends or family, especially when an eager young person is involved.

So if your best friend's uncle is a weather reporter for a local news station, chat with him at the next family gathering. Or ask your friend if you can get in touch with him to ask about internship or volunteer opportunities at the station. You may be left with a flat "no," or you may end up empty-handed after a few attempts, but you may also be pleasantly surprised. You'll never know what can happen until you reach out and give it a try. Even if your acquaintance doesn't have an opportunity at his or her organization, he or she may have other ideas or leads to offer you. Sometimes, just a little information is all you need to get going in the right direction.

## Ask for an Informational Interview

It may be easier than you think to learn about a career in movies or television. What better way to learn about something than to ask questions about it? If there is a television station or documentary filmmaker in your hometown, you might

be able to arrange an informational interview to discuss what the work is like. Even if the person you meet with does not have an opportunity in mind for you as an intern or volunteer, the interview will give you the chance to learn more about the field. An informational

Doing informational interviews, observing and shadowing professionals, or being an apprentice to someone with experience can be helpful in starting your career.

interview can be less pressured than a job interview because you are the one asking the questions. You may even find that the person you are interviewing loves to talk about his or her job!

Once you ask for and get an informational interview, take some time beforehand to prepare a list of questions. Think long and hard about the job and what you might want to know about it. For example, you might ask someone who works on films as a special effects artist about his or her training and how long it took to get the job. Questions about the person's typical workday can help you get an idea of daily life on the job. As part of the interview, you can ask for advice about the kinds of jobs someone your age might be able to do as an intern or volunteer.

Make your questions as thoughtful as possible, and try not to take too much of the person's time (about forty-five minutes should be enough). If done correctly, an informational interview can be a great tool for learning about the industry and where you can turn to find a television or film internship.

# Chapter Three

# THE WORLD OF TV

**E**ven though you may have been watching TV for your whole life, the behind-the-scenes world of television is probably unfamiliar to you. You may know all about the shows, commercials, and channels on television. You can name the TV stars who grace your living room every evening. However, navigating this world may be a bit of a tall order, especially when the world of television changes so frequently.

Television is a very popular and competitive industry. From the writers of sitcoms to the booking agents who send in the talent for auditions, the world of television can be competitive and high-stakes. But it does not have to be a harrowing experience to dip your toes into the industry's waters.

If you don't live in or near a major city, don't despair. You can explore what it is like to broadcast programming over the airwaves whether you live in a big city or a small town. While the major network TV stations such as ABC, NBC, and CBS in New York and Los Angeles have established internship

Staff in a television broadcast room work differently than film crews. The setup and procedures are more permanent for repeated broadcasts.

programs for college students, high school students are better off approaching smaller venues for break-through opportunities. In fact, smaller organizations may be more likely to give you hands-on involvement in a project. Three types of organizations to explore are local news stations, public broadcasting stations, and cable networks.

## Local News Stations

Local news stations can be found all across the United States and Canada. Tune into your local news to get an idea of where it is located. You may be able to research online where the station broadcasts from and if it has other offices besides its newsrooms. A local station may be designated to cover news in a certain number of counties or provinces. Identify the station that covers your own area because it will be the closest place for you to travel to.

After you have located the news offices, call or write a letter to find out more. If you are not answering a specific advertisement for help, explain why you are writing and where you go to school. Be clear that you are in high school and are looking for your first experience at a local station.

You may also find the local news represented at state fairs, career days, or other public events. These may even be some of the places where interns or volunteers are asked to work so that the

# Position Yourself for the Future

**Major networks usually do not offer opportunities for students as young as high school age, but if you've already done work at another type of television station, you will likely be high on their list of interns to choose for a college opportunity. So if you want to work for NBC, for example, remember that you may be able to get there by starting at your hometown TV station when you are in high school.**

station's presence becomes known throughout the community. Use these kinds of events to learn as much as you can about what the company does and how people can get jobs there.

At a news station, the on-air personalities and journalists broadcast the news and interview people, but there are many people working behind the scenes to help make that happen. Writers and researchers get the news from news services and by contacting the people involved in a story. They double-check facts before airing them, and they may cover international, national, and local news in the same broadcast.

In addition to the journalists who put together news stories, there are people who film the segments, edit the stories, and coordinate the sound and music to be used during the broadcasts. A news producer works to coordinate the efforts between journalists and sound, lighting, film crews, and even the makeup and wardrobe departments.

Staff that work at local news stations often have experience in journalism, history, film and video, editing, and writing. Local stations usually have live broadcasts a few times a day, but people work to prepare the news in the studio and on location throughout the day.

# Public Broadcasting Stations

Public broadcasting stations are located in small and large cities. These stations usually have commercial-free programing scheduled continuously throughout the day and night. The early-morning and late-afternoon hours often have programming for children who are home from school. During other hours, educational programming for adults is often broadcast. Areas such as current events, history, and culture are often the focus of public broadcasts for adults.

What sets public broadcasting apart from other kinds of television is the way that it is financed. A public station does not use advertising to raise money to run the station. Instead, it relies on donations from the public, often collected during fund-raising events such as pledge drives and telethons. Fund-raising is a large part of the public broadcasting system, and public stations often need volunteers and interns to help with membership and promotional events.

One way to get involved in public broadcasting is to watch your local station or check its Web site for station events. Then inquire about these events to see if help is needed to get them organized or set up. You may find that some volunteer help is welcomed. Even if you are just setting up chairs or handing out pamphlets at the door, you are becoming more familiar with the happenings of the station and what it is like to work in that environment.

Public broadcasting stations, which air educational shows like PBS's *Sesame Street*, may use more volunteers or interns than broadcast television stations.

At a public broadcasting station, you will likely run into people with backgrounds in journalism, music, art, education, and children's programming. There will likely be a large variety of programming to learn about and many people to meet. Experiences like these can be different from one day to the next. They can give you a wide view of the field and what it might have to offer you in the future.

## Cable Networks

If you are lucky enough to live in a city that has offices of cable networks, you may want to try interning or volunteering there. Some

# Big Cities, Big Opportunities

New York and Los Angeles are the most popular places to go to college for opportunities in movies and TV, but other areas, such as Chicago and Toronto, are popular, too. Keep this in mind when choosing a college. If you already live in these areas, you may be lucky enough to find an opportunity at one of the bigger television stations or movie companies while still in high school. Remember that the bigger the city you live in, the more of a chance you will have to work for a major company. You will also have a wider array of smaller organizations to explore.

cable TV stations are large and may not offer opportunities to young people. Others, such as public access stations, can be a great place to get more hands-on experience than you might get at other television stations.

Small, local, public access stations often have shows that are broadcast to educate the public about local issues, entertain the public with local performances, or promote local programs in libraries and schools. You may be surprised to find that everyday citizens

Production coordinators from the Tampa Bay Community Network, a public access station, monitor an interview with a high school athletic coach.

serve as camera crews and organize local shows. Contact your closest cable network office to find out what kinds of shows it has and how you can get involved.

Unlike public broadcasting stations, cable network stations rely on money they get from advertisements. One of the key jobs at a cable network is selling advertising; this is another area of the business that you might explore.

Looking into as many jobs as possible is a great way to learn about the field of television. Internships for academic credit will often provide an overview of several different departments at a station. Volunteers are more likely to work on particular events or projects, which will be completed or aired by a certain date.

# Chapter Four

# THE WORLD OF MOVIES

The movie industry makes billions of dollars a year. It is one of the biggest entertainment industries in the world. People love to go to the movies and get lost in the world of drama, action, comedy, science fiction, and fantasy.

The world of movies looks glamorous and fun, and many people are drawn to it. However, what sets apart the best workers from others? It is often a combination of talent, experience, and knowledge. People who get an early start learning about the business may have a better chance to stand out in these areas. A resourceful high school student may get just enough of a foot in the door by doing an internship or volunteer work in the movie industry.

While you may not go straight to Hollywood to work on a blockbuster film, you can take a more realistic route. Check out one of the following smaller venues, where you can have a chance to learn the trade.

Hundreds of people work on a movie, and the payoff is when it opens to the public in theaters. Here, fans line up for a midnight screening of *The Hunger Games* in New York.

## Documentary Film Companies

Documentary films are nonfiction features about real-world topics. The filmmakers do extensive research about a topic and may spend months or even years gathering the interviews and footage that they

Modern equipment allows these filmmakers and performers to view their work by playing back recordings on the set.

need to tell the story. Working with a documentary film company may involve scouting for locations to film or finding people to interview and setting up those interviews.

Someone exploring documentary filmmaking as a career may be interested in journalism or history. They are usually not as interested in the fictional storytelling, special effects, or blockbuster aspects of filmmaking. Documentary films are often made on a limited budget with a small crew of people. For this reason, documentary film companies are more likely to accept help from an unpaid intern or an eager volunteer.

The steps in a documentary project are similar to those in other film or television productions. However, instead of actors and scripts, a lot of the on-camera work involves location filming and interviewing. Documentary filmmakers usually have very portable equipment and cameras so that they can follow subjects around in a car, into buildings, or anywhere they want to go. Thorough research is always needed for documentary films, including checking the information that subjects give during their interviews.

Film editing is another important aspect of documentary filmmaking. While interviews with a subject may take hours and cover a lot of material, they are seldom used in the order in which they were shot. Clips from several interviews are often edited together when covering a certain topic, and location shots are interspersed between them so that a complete story can be told.

A documentary filmmaker may be interested in working with a student who has good grades and is an independent and hard worker. To prove that you possess these qualities, you may want to show a filmmaker any large projects that you have completed independently. Proving that you are interested and want to help can be half the battle.

## Specialty Production Companies

Like documentary film companies, there are other film companies that are located all around the world. The largest ones are in Los Angeles and New York, but there are plenty of smaller ones across the country. A smaller, specialty production company might be hired by a larger one to do filming, editing, sound production, or even

A production and camera crew records content for the reality Web series *If I Can Dream*, which is streamed online.

stunt work. One production company does not have to do everything associated with a film if it can hire a specialty production company to focus on a certain aspect, such as location shots or special effects. These companies may work with the director to provide the sets, costumes, makeup, or even the catering for employees or the tutoring of young children on the set. Animal trainers, voice coaches, and even human resources employees are needed to make a production company work. Sometimes, a production company may be created solely for the purpose of providing a specialized task. For example, the special effects company Industrial Light and Magic, created by

# Learning on Your Own

Remember that it is important to learn on your own in addition to learning on the job. If you are working at a production company and you are running errands for the director or casting agents but what you are really interested in is filming, you may need to practice those skills on your own time. When you are at the job, be helpful to the project. Then take your new knowledge and inspiration home with you and concentrate on what you like best. Remember that an internship or volunteer opportunity is often meant to help you make contacts and a good impression. You can do that by making sure to do what is expected of you on the job.

George Lucas's Lucasfilm, helps many other companies produce their special effects.

While a movie is being filmed, there are many people running around a set doing their work. But there are also many months of preparation before the filming even begins. Locations and dates for the film crews and actors must be planned. Permits for filming must be obtained. Actors must rehearse, stages must be built, and camera crews must be coordinated. The tasks that take place during the planning stage of a film are known as preproduction. Many smaller film and video companies specialize in preproduction services. Other companies focus on postproduction services, such as editing and sound dubbing.

The best way to get noticed by a specialty production company is to put together a great portfolio of work that you may have done on your own or with other small film crews. Putting together and offering to show your portfolio will show your determination, creativity, and eagerness to learn.

## Special Effects Companies

You are probably familiar with films that use heavy special effects. Action-adventure, fantasy, and science-fiction films often use these magical illusions to tell their stories in the most dramatic way possible. Decades ago, special effects were much harder to produce. Filmmakers created models of spaceships, hanging them with strings to make them look like they were flying. Nonhuman characters were actors wearing costumes. The lifelike images of computer-generated imagery (CGI), including characters such as Golem from *Lord of the Rings*, were not possible to create many years ago. But today, computer animation is changing the face of special effects.

Special effects crews and stunt crews worked to create this scene from *Transformers: Dark of the Moon.*

Jobs in special effects are perhaps the most coveted and mysterious in the film industry. Computer animators need a great deal of technical training and a lot of patience to create the scenes that they work on. On a big-budget Hollywood film, it may take an entire crew with scores of people to do the special effects.

Companies that specialize in this work may be located anywhere in the country. They are often hired by larger film production companies to do this specialized work. They may or may not be present on the set during the traditional filming. Their work often enhances the look of a scene, such as making it look like the action is taking place on another planet. Today's special effects can be accomplished much more easily, quickly, and cheaply than developing a full set that looks like a burned-out castle or a crowded coliseum. The technologies used in special effects have changed the film industry and the way actors and directors work on the set.

If you have ever experimented with special effects on your home computer or with a home video camera, you have an idea of what special effects can do. Today, computer programs can create effects such as explosions and car crashes. Creating a small video with special effects to put in a portfolio can help show your enthusiasm and determination. In addition, any personal projects; school productions; stage crew involvement, such as in lighting or sound; or other proof of your artistic or technical abilities can be a benefit when you look for an internship or volunteer opportunity. Remember, the people who show the greatest willingness to learn and the most persistence are the most likely to get the opportunities they seek. And there is no better opportunity than to work on a real production, no matter what it is.

# Chapter Five

# WORKING IN THE BUSINESS

**W**hen you watch a movie or TV show, you are seeing the finished product. Remember that there are numerous people involved in productions, from the writers who sell their scripts to the companies that gather the actors and crew. There are also many smaller companies and related agencies that serve the film and television industry. Don't forget to check out these opportunities as you explore jobs in the field. There are three particular areas that help support the movie and film industry. Movie studios, talent agencies, and casting companies are places that young people can explore if they are interested in getting a more complete picture of the industry.

## Movie Studios

Large movie studios can be like huge cities unto themselves. Not only are there countless office jobs to learn about, but there are also many chances to meet directly with the public and interact with other movie buffs. Movie studio tours are a big business in Los Angeles, and interns are often given interesting jobs to do in this area. Tours, working in gift shops, or helping out with special events can be a great way to get involved.

While some opportunities may be reserved for local college students, learning about these opportunities now can set you up for the future. Even if there are no opportunities for you immediately, or you are too young to take advantage of them in high school, it still helps to write to a human resources department at a studio. You may be provided with valuable information about where you can apply in the future and what the jobs for young people may entail.

Tourists visit the Diagon Alley set during the Harry Potter tour at Warner Brothers Leavesden Studios in London. Some TV and movie buffs work at movie studios.

One of the purposes of maintaining large movie studios is to provide tours and publicity to the public. California and Florida have some movie studios that are solely for the public's enjoyment. They provide a lot of movie nostalgia, demonstrations of special effects, and even rides and tours of studio lots. People on the tours can see sets used in popular movies and enjoy the atmosphere of the bustling film industry. These studios are important for relating to the public and giving the studio a fun image. People who enjoy communicating with others would enjoy this type of job. Even just volunteering at one-time events can be a good way to become familiar with the studios and their work.

## Talent Agencies

These busy agencies represent the talent that you see on television and in the movies. They often juggle many clients at a time, meeting with clients and their lawyers about the actors' various contracts. The back-end part of the business can be fascinating, especially for anyone interested in the legal rights of actors and movie studios.

The work of talent agents involves going to a lot of performances to analyze the work of actors, singers, or dancers. When a person's performance impresses them, they may decide to represent that person. The "talent" actually pays a fee to the agency to represent him or her. This representation makes the performer more visible to casting companies that are looking for people to work on films or television shows.

The talent agency must make sure that the talent is well represented with posed portrait photographs called headshots, video clips, or other information that can help get the performer a job. The

Pet talent agent Cris Rankin (right) holds up a treat so Frank the dog will stay and pose for pictures. The agency she co-owns, A1 Animal Talent, helps cast pets in TV commercials, films, and print ads.

agency also keeps track of its clients' talents and abilities. When an actor is needed who has a special skill, such as ice skating or driving a car, the talent agency should be able to find the right person to audition for the part.

Many talent agents work on commission. When the actor or other talent gets work, the talent agent will get a small percentage of that money. The commission works as payment for finding the person a job.

Someone who is interested in viewing a lot of performances, or in learning how legal issues affect the entertainment industry, may enjoy working at a talent agency.

## Casting Companies

Casting companies work hand-in-hand with talent agencies. A casting company works with a movie studio or production company to provide the talent needed for a production. A director or producer may contact a casting company to find particular kinds of actors, such as young children who can sing, older men who can type, or young women who can swim. Nearly any request can be made to a talent agency! The casting company's job is to find people who have the physical look of the characters and any special talents

# Make Your Own Opportunities

**Volunteering can give a person a certain amount of freedom. If an organization has no established internship program and you are not concerned about getting school credit for your efforts, you may be able to create the opportunity that you are looking for by volunteering. Find out if you are allowed to volunteer in a particular department in a film company that interests you. A volunteer may have a greater ability to concentrate on the area of his or her choice.**

or skills needed to act the parts. (Of course, the right actor may win a role and then later learn a new skill required for the part.)

A casting company will set up casting calls and auditions for parts in a movie or television show. After the right actor is chosen for the role, the talent's fee is negotiated and contracts are drafted. An actor must follow the provisions of the contract in order to get paid. For this reason, lawyers and other people who are familiar with contracts and law often work at casting companies.

Casting a production can take a long time, especially if a director is very particular about the talent that he or she wants for important roles. A casting company must also be able to work fast, especially in cases in which an actor must be replaced quickly. The casting company is paid directly by the movie studio.

Most casting companies are located in big cities where production studios are located, but they may also travel to smaller cities looking for talent. This may be the case if a movie will be on location in a smaller city for an extended period of time. Keep a lookout in trade magazines for possible films that may come on location to your city. If a casting company is looking for local extras, it may

A casting call includes information about the kind of talent needed for a particular production. The casting company sends the right talent to the auditions.

need help from local volunteers to keep casting calls running smoothly. Check around, ask questions, and see how you can get involved.

# Chapter Six

# WORKING ALONG WITH THE BUSINESS

**Y**ou've learned about jobs that are done on the sets of movies, behind the scenes, and in offices around the country. But you haven't yet explored all the possible ways that a TV or movie buff can get involved in the business. There are many ways that people can learn about the industry while not actually working at a television studio or on a movie set. Reading industry publications is an important way for people to keep up with what is going on in the business. Film institutes and museums pay tribute to the industry and offer a historical look at television and film. Advertising is a big part of television and is itself a huge industry. Interns and volunteers can get involved in all of these parts of the business and learn about what they might enjoy.

## Industry Publications

Industry publications help people in television and movie careers get news about their industry. Magazines and other periodicals give information about developments in the business, including which director has signed on to direct which film, who is producing it, and which television pilots have been signed by which networks. Blogs and Internet sites can also be sources of this kind of information. Industry magazines, blogs, and Web sites are great places to learn about the film and television industries, as well as the publishing industry.

Local and state newspapers typically have arts and entertainment sections that explore the entertainment industry. Film reviews are one of the most prominent features of this section of the newspaper. Film reviewers do exactly what you would expect. They go to see many movies and then report about each one. While a teen may not get a job like this while still in high school, there is a lot that a high school student can do to make his or her writing visible. School newspapers may offer space for film reviews. Starting your own blog is another way to make your voice on films heard.

If you are interested in working in the field with professionals, however, contact local magazines or newspapers that provide news about the film or television industry. Smaller papers may be willing to offer working opportunities to young people who show an interest. Some internship programs with newspapers may already be established. If this is the case, you may want to specify that you would like to work on arts and entertainment because you are planning for a career in that area.

When you are on the job, try to be as helpful, focused, and alert as possible. The information you learn on the job can be useful for years to come.

# Film Institutes and Museums

Film institutes and museums are more common than you may think. Small and large film collections are located around the country in the

# Choose a Mentor

**A mentor is an experienced professional who agrees to help teach you what you need to know about the field.** No matter what part of the television or movie business you find yourself interning or volunteering in, having a mentor is a great way to learn. You can benefit from your mentor's experience and wisdom, and ask questions about issues you find challenging. A mentor can provide a recommendation for college and can review your personal projects and offer feedback.

A mentor can teach you about the business and introduce you to other people who may be able to help, too.

form of institutes, museums, and even traveling collections at larger museums.

If you have one of these collections near your home, ask if you can help out. As an intern or volunteer, you may communicate with the public that comes to see the memorabilia or learn about the history of film. You may have the chance to learn about older technologies that are no longer in use. Museums often use volunteers because a lot of their funding relies on donations from the public. This can give you a good opportunity to get involved and help when and how you want to.

Museum director Jeffrey Pipes Guice helps prepare a film memorabilia collection for display at the Louisiana Film Museum in New Orleans.

## Advertising Firms

You have probably seen thousands of commercials in your lifetime. You may know that
some commercials are put together like a
film, with expensive budgets and special
effects. National commercials are usually
made by large advertising firms in large cities. But there are also plenty of small firms
that make local television commercials.
These firms may be family-owned, or they
may be very small production houses that
service small businesses in the area. You
may have seen low-budget commercials
for local car dealers, restaurants, jewelers,
or pet stores. The agencies that make these
commercials may offer great opportunities
for young people to get involved in some
aspect of production.

If you are lucky enough to live in or near
a big city with larger advertising firms, you
can learn about the kinds of jobs people do
at an advertising agency. These are great
places to write letters asking for an informational interview with an employee.

There are many aspects of advertising,
and people usually specialize in just one.
There are people who develop the ideas and write the scripts and
others who book the talent or schedule the productions. Other workers decide where the commercials will air and how much will be paid

Creating commercials involves many of the same skills as making films or television shows. There may be volunteer or internship opportunities in local advertising firms.

for the time. Get in on the ground floor now, and you may be able to climb to more responsible jobs in time. Each commercial project has its own schedule, and you may be asked to do different tasks on different commercials.

# Think About a Paying Job, Too

If you are having trouble finding an internship or volunteer opportunity in the film or television field and you are old enough for a paying job, consider working at a movie theater or playhouse. Even the people who sell the tickets or clean the theaters can have a chance to see how movie reels are changed, how films are delivered, and how films and performances are promoted. You may be able to see the films or performances for free while you are at it!

# Chapter Seven

# MAKING THE MOST OF YOUR INTERNSHIP OR VOLUNTEER OPPORTUNITY

An internship opportunity can have a great effect on a young person. It may influence where you go to school and what you major in. If you enjoy your internship or volunteer job, you may decide to look for colleges with strong programs in communications and the arts. You may want to become a film major or learn about writing for television. As you intern or volunteer, ask people where they went to college and what they majored in. You will find that there are many good programs out there. However, you may also find that many people did not attend programs in film or communications. Many people may have learned "on the job" instead.

Getting involved, asking questions, and absorbing new information can help you get the career you want. It can also help you eliminate jobs that you thought you wanted before seeing the day-to-day reality.

# Be an Intern of Life

Whether or not you are completing your ideal internship, keep reading and learning about the parts of the industry that interest you. A local library may have trade magazines in which you can read about TV or film. Become a regular reader of these trade magazines to learn about the individuals and companies that may offer you opportunities when you are older.

## Doing the Intern's Job

When working as a volunteer or intern, don't worry if you are asked to do some boring tasks. You can't expect to direct a television show or cast a leading actor in a role on day one. The work of an intern is often thankless and unglamorous. But make the most of your experience by learning as much as you can about the process. For example, you may be asked to stuff envelopes or help clean a dressing room or catering table. Find out what you are stuffing into the envelopes and what the mailing is about. Learn about the special makeup used on the air when you are helping in the dressing room. Be alert, ask questions, and be curious. Use the opportunity to observe what other professionals are doing and decide what you think about

News and other TV productions need crews to work in many areas, including hair and makeup.

the business itself. That is more important than the nature of the tasks you are doing right now.

Always be on the lookout for opportunities to break new ground. If you spend time in an internship and get ideas about how some tasks could be done in the future, you can certainly talk to someone about it. Look for someone who seems open to new ideas and respectful of the work that interns do. This may be a good person to choose as a mentor. In this way, you can learn new things and have someone to share ideas with.

## Making a Portfolio

You may not realize how valuable your internship is until you start to apply to colleges or look for other job opportunities. An internship or volunteer experience can look very impressive on a résumé or college application. It demonstrates that you are focused on your goals and

Making a digital portfolio is a terrific way to highlight your accomplishments in the field.

are willing to pursue opportunities that will help you learn. That may cause someone viewing your application to choose you over other students.

In addition to describing your experience on paper, making a portfolio is a great way to show a prospective school or employer what you can do. Artists make portfolios by making a book of prints of their artwork. But someone who has worked in film or television may need another kind of portfolio to show his or her work. If you have had experiences in which you have helped create film or video, a digital portfolio is the best way to showcase the work that you have done.

You can make a digital portfolio on a DVD or even on a Web site. Be sure to include information about what you specifically did on each project so that the person viewing it can understand your role. This will also make it clear that you are not trying to claim that you did something that you didn't. If you ran the cameras, participated in making sound effects, or helped edit, list those accomplishments separately and with a description or audio commentary. Provide the name of the director or other person in charge of your work. If he or she agrees, that person can be contacted to verify your accomplishments or give a recommendation.

In addition to including examples of work associated with your internship, be sure to include any individual projects that you completed on your own. This can give the viewer an instant understanding of what you can do and your level of creativity. Try to show a variety of work in your portfolio. You can include work that you did for school projects, art classes, and paid or volunteer jobs. Remember to include only your very best work, even if it means only including a few pieces. Avoid including too many examples of the same kind of work. Also try to leave out personal projects that you needed a lot of help from someone else to do. This will not give someone an accurate idea of what you can do independently.

A DVD or Web site portfolio is great because it can be sent or accessed easily. With a digital portfolio, you do not have to send a heavy book through the mail and you can combine moving pictures, still pictures, and a written or audio description of your work. Some schools' art departments or guidance offices can help you put together a digital portfolio if you ask.

A digital portfolio can even be a tool to help you get an internship. Some companies may want to see what you can do. Then, after you have worked as an intern or volunteer, you can update your portfolio and résumé to include the work that you did during your experience with the organization. Remember that your portfolio will have to be constantly updated for years to show your latest projects. Each time you update it, you can remove any earlier work that you no longer feel represents your abilities. Even people who have been working in the film and television industries for decades update their portfolios and résumés on a regular basis.

Work on your portfolio carefully, and get someone to review your work with you. It is important to do the best job you can and make your work look as professional as possible. While it is true that you are sending your portfolio and résumé to people to try to get experience in the field, it helps to show what you have already accomplished.

## Feel Encouraged

Internships and volunteer opportunities in your community are a great first step to jump-starting a career. Whether or not you get your dream internship, you can always begin learning about the film or television industry on your own. You can feel encouraged that you have specific goals in mind and are already taking steps to reach them. Read periodicals about the industry, read books about great films and filmmakers, write movie reviews, write or film your own productions with friends, or do any other thing that gets you excited about the film or television industry. By simply taking these steps to learn, you'll get a head start on becoming an insider in the exciting field of TV and movies.

# Glossary

**academic credit**  Recognition by a college or school that a student has fulfilled a requirement leading to a degree.

**broadcasting station**  A television station that provides programming transmitted through traditional broadcast methods.

**cable network**  A television network that provides programming transmitted through underground cable network lines.

**casting company**  A company that searches for talent to be used in television, on stage, or in film productions.

**computer-generated imagery (CGI)**  Animated graphics produced by a computer and then used in film or television.

**director**  A person who has artistic control of a film or television show, guiding the performances of the actors, the cinematography, and other aspects of production.

**documentary**  A film or video that uses factual records and interviews to report on a topic and tell a true story.

**film institute**  An organization that is dedicated to movies, their creation, and their history, and is usually open to the public.

**informational interview**  An interview with a professional designed to gather information and details about working in a profession and breaking into the field.

**intern**  A student or trainee who works in an occupation for a certain period of time, usually without pay and sometimes for academic credit.

**journalist**  A person who writes for newspapers or magazines, or who broadcasts news on television or radio.

**periodical**  A magazine, newspaper, or journal that is published on a regular basis.

**pilot**  A first episode of a television program created as a test for the network to decide whether to proceed with regular production.

**portfolio**  A collection of creative works that showcase a person's skills, often used by individuals seeking employment or school admission.

**producer**  A person or group that is responsible for the financial and logistical aspects of making a film or television program.

**public broadcasting station**  A broadcasting network or station that is designed to serve and educate the public and is supported by public donations and financial grants.

**résumé**  A document that lists a person's education, qualifications, and previous work experiences.

**talent agency**  An agency that represents performing artists and promotes them for work in performances, film, and television.

**volunteer**  To work for an organization without pay.

# For More Information

Academy of Canadian Cinema & Television (ACCT)
49 Ontario Street, Suite 501
Toronto ON M5A 2V1
Canada
(416) 366-2227
Web site: http://www.academy.ca
The ACCT works to heighten public awareness and increase audience
attendance and appreciation of Canadian film and television
productions. It also provides high-quality and creative professional
development programs.

Academy for Careers in Television & Film (ACTVF)
36-41 28th Street
Long Island City, NY 11106
(718) 472-0536
Web site: http://www.actvf.org
This public high school in Queens, New York, offers a college
preparatory curriculum along with meaningful preparation for
careers in television and film production. Industry internships
and hands-on experiences allow students to develop the technical skills and work habits necessary to successfully pursue
careers in production.

Academy of Television Arts & Sciences Foundation
Student Internship Program
5220 Lankershim Boulevard

North Hollywood, CA 91601-3109

Web site: http://www.emmysfoundation.org/internship-programs

This charitable foundation works to preserve and celebrate the history of television and educate those who will shape its future. Its internship program gives students in-depth exposure to professional television production during an eight-week summer period in Los Angeles.

American Cinema Editors (ACE)

100 Universal City Plaza

Verna Fields Building 2282, Room 190

Universal City, CA 91608

(818) 777-2900

Web site: http://ace-filmeditors.org

This honorary society of motion picture editors offers an internship program in Los Angeles for aspiring film and video editors.

American Film Institute (AFI)

2021 North Western Avenue

Los Angeles, CA 90027-1657

(323) 856-7600

Web site: http://www.afi.com

This nonprofit educational and cultural organization archives rare film footage and educates the public about America's film heritage.

American Society of Cinematographers (ACS)

P.O. Box 2230

Hollywood, CA 90078

(800) 448-0145

Web site: http://www.theasc.com

This nonprofit organization educates aspiring filmmakers and others about the art of cinematography. It publishes the well-respected magazine *American Cinematographer* and the *American Cinematographer Manual*.

Directors Guild of America (DGA)

7920 Sunset Boulevard

Los Angeles, CA 90046

(310) 289-2000

Web site: http://www.dga.org

The DGA represents professional directors and directorial staff working in film, television, commercials, documentaries, news, sports, and new media. The organization offers a program that trains participants to become assistant directors.

New York Film Academy (NYFA)

100 East 17th Street

New York, NY 10003

(212) 477-1414

Web site: http://www.nyfa.edu

The NYFA offers summer camp opportunities for teens interested in filmmaking, screenwriting, broadcast journalism, or 3-D animation.

Sundance Institute

P.O. Box 684429

Park City, UT 84068

(435) 658-3456

Web site: http://www.sundance.org

The Sundance Institute is a nonprofit organization dedicated to the discovery and development of independent artists and audiences in film and theater.

Vancouver Film School (VFS)

198 West Hastings Street

Vancouver, BC V6B 1H2

Canada

(604) 685-5808

Web site: http://www.vfs.com

One of Canada's leading film schools, the VFS offers courses and experiences in all aspects of filmmaking.

# Web Sites

Due to the changing nature of Internet links, Rosen Publishing has developed an online list of Web sites related to the subject of this book. This site is updated regularly. Please use this link to access the list:

http://www.rosenlinks.com/FID/TVM

# For Further Reading

Culver, Sherri Hope, and James A. Seguin. *Media Career Guide: Preparing for Jobs in the 21st Century*. 8th ed. Boston, MA: Bedford/St. Martin's, 2011.

Dunkleberger, Amy. *So You Want to Be a Film or TV Director?* (Careers in Film and Television). Berkeley Heights, NJ: Enslow, 2008.

Dunkleberger, Amy. *So You Want to Be a Film or TV Editor?* (Careers in Film and Television). Berkeley Heights, NJ: Enslow, 2008.

Ferguson Publishing. *Careers in Focus: Broadcasting*. 3rd ed. New York, NY: Ferguson's, 2007.

Ferguson Publishing. *Movies* (Discovering Careers). New York, NY: Ferguson's, 2012.

Friedman, Joshua A. *Getting It Done: The Ultimate Production Assistant Guide*. Studio City, CA: Michael Wiese Productions, 2011.

Gervich, Chad. *Small Screen, Big Picture: A Writer's Guide to the TV Business*. New York, NY: Three Rivers Press, 2008.

Grove, Elliot. *130 Projects to Get You into Filmmaking*. Hauppauge, NY: Barron's Educational Series, 2009.

Hamlett, Christina. *Screenwriting for Teens: The 100 Principles of Scriptwriting Every Budding Writer Must Know*. Studio City, CA: Michael Wiese Productions, 2006.

Hart, John. *The Art of the Storyboard: A Filmmaker's Introduction*. 2nd ed. Boston, MA: Elsevier/Focal Press, 2008.

Hays, Robin. *Career Diary of a Movie Producer: Thirty Days Behind the Scenes with a Professional* (Gardner's Career Diaries). Washington, DC: Garth Gardner, 2008.

Kirschner, Carole M. *Hollywood Game Plan: How to Land a Job in Film, TV, and Digital Entertainment*. Studio City, CA: Michael Wiese Productions, 2012.

Lenburg, Jeff. *Career Opportunities in Animation*. New York, NY: Ferguson's, 2012.

Murphy, Mary. *Beginner's Guide to Animation: Everything You Need to Know to Get Started*. New York, NY: Watson-Guptill, 2008.

Owens, Jim, and Gerald Millerson. *Video Production Handbook*. 5th ed. Burlington, MA: Focal Press, 2012.

Savoie, Michael P., and Frank Barnas. *Careers in Media*. 2nd ed. Boston, MA: Allyn & Bacon, 2010.

Scherzer, Mark, and Keith Fenimore. *Hire Me, Hollywood! Your Behind-the-Scenes Guide to the Most Exciting—and Unexpected—Jobs in Show Business*. Avon, MA: Adams Media, 2011.

Schneider, Steven Jay. *501 Movie Directors: A Comprehensive Guide to the Greatest Filmmakers*. Hauppauge, NY: Barron's Educational Series, 2007.

Segall, Miriam. *Career Building Through Digital Moviemaking* (Digital Career Building). New York, NY: Rosen Publishing, 2008.

Suber, Howard. *Letters to Young Filmmakers: Creativity & Getting Your Films Made*. Studio City, CA: Michael Wiese Productions, 2011.

Thompson, Lisa. *Going Live in 3, 2, 1: Have You Got What It Takes to Be a TV Producer?* Minneapolis, MN: Compass Point Books, 2009.

Wise, Carolyn C. *Vault Guide to Top Internships*. 2009 ed. New York, NY: Vault, 2008.

# Bibliography

Aksomitis, Linda. *Choosing a Career* (Issues That Concern You). Farmington Hills, MI: Greenhaven Press, 2009.

Bolles, Richard Nelson, Carol Christen, and Jean M. Blomquist. *What Color Is Your Parachute? For Teens: Discovering Yourself, Defining Your Future*. Berkeley, CA: Ten Speed Press, 2006.

Breman, Phil. "How to Get an Entry Level Entertainment Job If You Have No Experience." About.com. Retrieved January 22, 2012 (http://filmtvcareers.about.com/od/gettingthejob/a/No_Experience.htm).

Breman, Phil. "How to Get a Production Internship." About.com. Retrieved January 22, 2012 (http://filmtvcareers.about.com/od/gettingthejob/a/HT_ProdIntern.htm).

Canadian Radio-Television and Telecommunications Commission. "Types of TV Broadcasters." October 4, 2009. Retrieved January 20, 2012 (http://www.crtc.gc.ca/eng/info_sht/b320.htm).

Coon, Nora. *Teen Dream Jobs: How to Get the Job You Really Want Now!* Hillsboro, OR: Beyond Words Publishing, 2003.

Eberts, Marjorie, and Margaret Gisler. *Careers for Culture Lovers & Other Artsy Types* (VGM Careers for You). 2nd ed. Chicago, IL: VGM Career Books, 1999.

Farr, J. Michael, and Laurence Shatkin. *250 Best Jobs Through Apprenticeships*. Indianapolis, IN: JIST Works, 2005.

Ferguson Publishing. *Careers in Focus: Arts & Entertainment*. 2nd ed. Chicago, IL: Ferguson's, 1999.

Goldberg, Jan. *Careers for Geniuses & Other Gifted Types* (VGM Careers for You). Chicago, IL: VGM Career Books, 2001.

Jaen, Rafael. *Show Case: Developing, Maintaining, and Presenting a Design-Tech Portfolio for Theatre and Allied Fields*. 2nd ed. Waltham, MA: Focal Press, 2012.

Lilly, Destiny. "Casting Directors vs. Talent Agents." Casting in the City, April 27, 2011. Retrieved January 27, 2012 (http://destinycasting. wordpress.com/2011/04/27/casting-directors-vs-talent-agents).

O'Brien, Lisa, and Stephen MacEachern. *Lights, Camera, Action! Making Movies and TV from the Inside Out*. Toronto, ON, Canada: Maple Tree Press, 2007.

Sawicki, Mark. *Filming the Fantastic: A Guide to Visual Effects Cinematography*. 2nd ed. Waltham, MA: Focal Press, 2011.

Slate.com. "The Difference Between an 'Agent' and a 'Manager.'" December 8, 1998. Retrieved January 30, 2012 (http://www. slate.com/articles/news_and_politics/explainer/1998/12/the_ difference_between_an_agent_and_a_manager.html).

Wyckoff, Claire. *Top Careers in Two Years: Communications and the Arts*. New York, NY: Ferguson's, 2007.

# Index

# About the Author

Adam Furgang is a film buff who has always enjoyed watching movies and reading about the industry and his favorite filmmakers. He dabbles in filmmaking as a hobby when he is not busy writing. He has written a number of young adult books for Rosen Publishing. He lives in upstate New York with his wife and two sons.

# Photo Credits

Cover © iStockphoto.com/Nathan Jones; pp. 4–5 Hemera/Thinkstock; pp. 8–9 Windred Evers/Photonica/Getty Images; p. 10 Siri Stafford/Stone/Getty Images; p. 13 BananaStock/Thinkstock; p. 17 Digital Vision/Thinkstock; pp. 18–19 Goodshoot/Thinkstock; p. 21 Monashee Frantz/OJO Images/Getty Images; pp. 22–23 Alan Pappe/Photodisc/Getty Images; pp. 26–27 © iStockphoto.com/Anthony Brown; p. 30 © CTW/Courtesy Everett Collection; p. 32 © St. Petersburg Times/ZUMA Press; pp. 35, 48–49, 55, 56–57 © AP Images; pp. 36–37 VisitBritain/Jack Barnes/Britain On View/Getty Images; pp. 38–39 © Lisa Rose/ZUMA Press; pp. 42–43 © Paramount Pictures/Courtesy Everett Collection; p. 46 Dan Kitwood/Getty Images; p. 51 © Detroit Free Press/ZUMA Press; p. 54 Tony Anderson/Stone/Getty Images; p. 61 DreamPictures/The Image Bank/Getty Images; pp. 62–63 © iStockphoto.com/Arne Thaysen.

Designer: Michael Moy; Editor: Andrea Sclarow Paskoff;
Photo Researcher: Karen Huang